Health Care
FOR INFANTS
AND TODDLERS

by Kristin Thoennes Keller

Consultant:
Angela Thompson-Busch, MD, PhD
President/CEO
All About Children Pediatrics, PA
Eden Prairie, Minnesota

SKILLS
FOR
TEENS
WHO
PARENT

LifeMatters
an imprint of Capstone Press
Mankato, Minnesota

LifeMatters Books are published by Capstone Press
PO Box 669 • 151 Good Counsel Drive • Mankato, Minnesota 56002
http://www.capstone-press.com

SPECIAL ADVISORY: The information within this book concerns sensitive and important issues about which parental and teen discretion is advised. Because this book is general in nature, the reader should consult an appropriate health, medical, or other professional for advice. The publisher and its consultants take no responsibility for the use of any of the materials or methods described in this book nor for the products thereof.

Printed in the United States of America

Library of Congress Cataloging-in-Publication Data
Thoennes Keller, Kristin.
      Health care for infants and toddlers / by Kristin Thoennes Keller.
          p.   cm.—(Skills for teens who parent)
      Includes bibliographical references and index.
      ISBN 0-7368-0704-7 (book)
      1. Infants—Care—Juvenile literature. 2. Toddlers—Care—Juvenile literature. 3. Infants—Health and hygiene—Juvenile literature. 4. Toddlers—Health and hygiene—Juvenile literature.
      [1. Babies—Care. 2. Toddlers—Care. 3. Babies—Health and hygiene. 4. Toddlers—Health and hygiene. 5. Teenage parents.] I. Title. II. Series.
      RJ101.7 T47 2001
      618.92—dc21   00-030971
                                                      CIP

      Summary: Teaches how to deal with common childhood health problems, such as colds, croup, vomiting, diarrhea, poisoning, burns, head injuries, choking, and more; also includes signs, treatment, and prevention of these conditions.

Staff Credits
Rebecca Aldridge, editor; Adam Lazar, designer; Kim Danger, photo researcher

Photo Credits
Cover: PNI/©Rosanne Olson, large; Stock Market/©Jose Pelaz, top; middle; ©DigitalVision, bottom
©DigitalVision, 35
FPG International/©Jim Cummins, 44
International Stock/©Jeremy Scott, 38; ©Mitch Diamond, 53
©Kimberly Danger, 7
Photo Network/©Esbin-Anderson, 14, 49
©Stockbyte, 29
Unicorn Stock Photos/©Steve Bourgeois, 9; ©Tracy Siehndel Freeman, 20; ©Eric R. Berndt, 37; ©Aneal E. Vohra, 54
Uniphoto/©Jackson Smith, 10; ©Rick Brady, 30
Visuals Unlimited/©Rick Poley, 22; ©John D. Cunningham, 41; ©Eric Anderson, 47; ©Nancy R. Alexander, 57; ©SIU, 59

A 0 9 8 7 6 5 4 3 2 1

Table of Contents

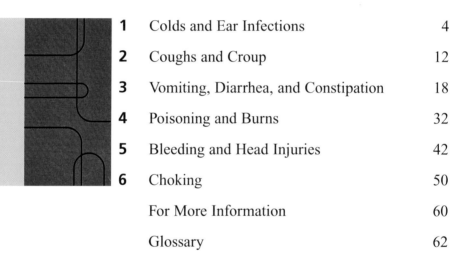

Chapter Overview

- Always call your doctor if you have questions about your child's health or safety.

- A cold is an upper respiratory infection. People catch colds from other people.

- At times, you may need to call the doctor when your child has cold symptoms.

- There is no cure for the common cold.

- Ear infections are painful. Call the doctor if your child has signs of an ear infection. Your child may need antibiotics.

CHAPTER 1

Colds and Ear Infections

Introduction

The recommendations in this book regarding your child's health and safety are guidelines for your information. The health care recommendations are not a substitute for a doctor's advice. The life-saving strategies discussed are not a substitute for information from a doctor or a first aid class. Always call your doctor if you have questions about your child's health or safety. You should take a class if you want to keep your child safe in life-threatening emergencies.

Colds

Colds are a common illness in children younger than 2. A cold is an upper respiratory infection. Tiny germs called viruses infect the lining of breathing passages. These passages are in the nose, throat, ears, sinuses, and bronchi in the lungs. The lining reacts by producing a sticky liquid called mucus. A person with a cold often has a runny nose or cough.

People usually catch colds from other people. Your child may breathe in after someone with a cold has sneezed or coughed. Sometimes children catch colds indirectly. This happens when someone with a cold transfers the virus to his or her own hand. This person then touches the hand of a healthy person. The healthy person then touches his or her own nose, mouth, or eyes and catches the cold.

Typical cold symptoms should gradually disappear after 3 to 4 days.

Signs of a Cold

Colds usually have many familiar symptoms. One sign of a cold can be a runny nose that begins with clear mucus which becomes thicker and slightly colored. Another sign is a slight fever of 101 to 102 degrees Fahrenheit (F) (38.3 to 38.9 degrees Celsius [C]). The fever usually occurs in the evening. Other cold symptoms include coughing, irritability, decreased appetite, slightly swollen glands, a sore throat or difficulty swallowing, and sneezing.

When to Call the Doctor

If your child is 3 months or younger, call the doctor at the first sign of illness. The cold could quickly turn into something more serious. For a child older than 3 months, call the doctor if your child has these symptoms:

- Clear mucus that becomes thick, runny, and green

- Cough that lasts longer than 1 week

- Difficulty breathing

- Ear pain

- Fever higher than 102 degrees F (38.9 degrees C)

- Excessive sleepiness or crankiness (anger that occurs easily)

- Blue lips or fingernails

- Difficulty eating or drinking

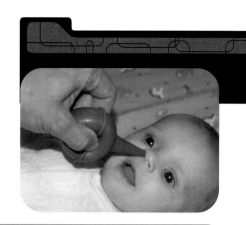

"When Ethan was a baby, I called the doctor all the time when he had a cold. Now I know better. I just watch Ethan's symptoms. Usually he gets better on his own. Sometimes, though, the symptoms get worse. That's when I call our doctor."

Treatment for Colds

The common cold has no cure. You can, however, try to make your child comfortable. The following tips can help:

- Offer extra fluids and make sure he gets extra rest.

- Give acetaminophen or ibuprofen for fever. Follow your doctor's recommendations for the correct amount of these medicines. Don't give aspirin, which has been linked to a serious condition called Reye syndrome.

- Don't offer any over-the-counter, or nonprescription, cold medicines without talking with your doctor.

- Place a cool-mist humidifier in your child's room. This device keeps air damp and moist. Clean and dry the humidifier each day.

- Clear your baby's nose by withdrawing fluid with a bulb syringe. If your doctor suggests it, place a few saline drops in each nostril before using the syringe. Saline is a liquid made of salt and water.

- Two-thirds of all children have at least one ear infection by their second birthday.

- Children in day care get more ear infections than children cared for at home.

- Infants who self-feed while lying on their back tend to get ear infections.

Prevention for Colds

The best way to prevent colds is to keep your baby away from people who have them. This is difficult when your child is in day care. Teach your child to wash his hands often and not to touch his face. Teach him to cough and sneeze into his elbow and always to use a tissue.

Ear Infections

Ear infections are another common childhood illness. They can happen when fluid gathers in the middle ear during colds and upper respiratory infections. Sometimes bacteria infect the fluid. Then pain and inflammation, or redness, heat, and swelling, occur.

Ear infections are most common during winter and early spring. Children who have summertime infections probably have infections of the outer ear canal. This is called swimmer's ear. This book, however, focuses on middle ear infections.

Signs of an Ear Infection

Your child may have an ear infection if you notice these signs:

- Crankiness

- Frequent nighttime waking

- Change in sleep patterns

- Crying or screaming with cold symptoms

- Sudden worsening of a cold

- Crying while lying flat

- Eye drainage

- Increasingly thick mucus from the nose

- Difference in sucking (in breastfed babies)

- Tugging at ears, face, and neck

Ear pulling isn't always an indication of ear infection. Most babies pull at their ears as they discover their own body. Also, babies often pull at their ears because of teething.

When to Call the Doctor

If you notice the previous signs in your baby, call the doctor. Don't wait. Ear infections are painful and need medical treatment.

Treatment for Ear Infections

If an ear is infected, your child's doctor may prescribe an oral antibiotic. Usually, this treatment that is taken by mouth lasts 10 days. Symptoms should improve within 3 days. Call the doctor if you don't see improvement in 3 days. Your child may need a different antibiotic.

It's important that your child finish all of the medicine unless directed not to by the doctor. This is true even if your child feels better before finishing the bottle. Some of the bacteria that caused the infection may still be present. Stopping the medicine too soon can allow the infection to return.

You can help keep your child comfortable by giving the doctor's recommended amount of acetaminophen or ibuprofen. If your child has a fever, don't overdress her.

If your child is feeling well, she can go to day care with an ear infection. The caregiver should give the medicine so your child doesn't miss any doses.

Preventing Ear Infections

Occasional ear infections can't be prevented. But some children get one after another. If so, doctors may suggest antibiotics during the whole winter season. This usually reduces the number of infections. Sometimes children get repeat ear infections from allergies.

Some children continue getting ear infections even while taking an antibiotic. These children may need tubes put in their ears that allow fluid to drain from the middle ear.

How to Give Medicine to an Infant

Using a medicine dropper is best. Make sure to measure the medicine correctly in either teaspoons or milliliters. One teaspoon equals five milliliters. Have the dropper filled and nearby. Cradle your child's head in the crook of your arm. With that arm, encircle your child's cheek. Gently pull out the corner of his mouth with your middle or index finger. With the other hand, slowly drop the medicine into the pocket that's formed. Allow time for him to swallow. If your child spits up the entire dose right away, you can repeat it. However, if your child continues to spit up or vomit, call your doctor.

You can do a few things at home to help prevent ear infections. Try to avoid contact with people who have a respiratory illness. Teach your child to wash her hands and not touch her face. If your infant is bottlefeeding, keep her in a semi-upright position to feed. This reduces the chance of fluid buildup in her ears. Whether in a house or car, people shouldn't smoke around your child. Secondhand smoke that a smoker blows out can lead to ear infections.

POINTS TO CONSIDER

When should you call the doctor for your child's cold? How can you treat a cold at home?

What are some signs that your child may have an ear infection?

Why is it important to give your child all of the antibiotic your doctor prescribes?

- Coughs usually are connected to respiratory illnesses. Many things can cause coughs.

- Coughs often are not treated with medication. However, there are times when you should call your doctor for your child's cough.

- Croup is a serious cough that can cut off a child's air supply.

- You can help your child through an episode of croup. If the episode is bad, take your child to an emergency room.

CHAPTER 2

Coughs and Croup

Coughs

Coughing is common among infants and toddlers. This is because young children often catch upper respiratory illnesses. Coughs usually are connected to respiratory illnesses. Coughing almost always is a sign that your child's air passages are irritated. Nerve endings in the lungs, throat, or windpipe sense the irritation. A reflex then causes air to be ejected, or driven, forcefully through the air passages.

Allergies also can cause coughs because mucus drips down the back of the throat. This produces a dry cough that's hard to stop. This cough is stronger at night. Children who cough only at night may have asthma. See the LifeMatters book *Asthma* for more information.

Coughs can occur for other reasons as well. Temporary irritants can cause coughs. These bothersome substances might include paint fumes or tobacco smoke. Coughs also can occur when a child is spitting up.

When to Call the Doctor

If your child is younger than 2 months and develops a cough, call your doctor right away. For older infants and children, call your doctor if:

- The cough lasts longer than 1 week.

- The cough begins suddenly and stays, and you feel something may be lodged in your child's throat.

- The coughing makes breathing difficult for your child.

- The coughing is painful, ongoing, and accompanied by a whooping or barking sound or vomiting.

- The coughing causes your child to turn blue.

- The cough brings up thick, yellowish-green mucus.

- The cough keeps your child awake at night.

Treatment for Coughs

If it's necessary to bring your child to the doctor, he or she will try to determine the cough's cause. The doctor will listen to your child's lungs. Treatment for a cough depends on its cause. Usually a doctor suggests extra fluids and rest. Your doctor may prescribe medicine if there's an infection. Never use over-the-counter medicine unless your doctor recommends it.

Some doctors suggest using telephone books to slightly raise the mattress where your child would lay her head. Lifting the mattress slightly raises your child's head and chest while she sleeps. This can help her breathing.

You can help treat your child's cough at home. Give her extra fluids. Run a cool-mist humidifier to keep the air moist. Make sure your child gets plenty of rest.

Some coughs are nothing to worry about. You probably don't need to worry if:

- The cough is steadily improving.

- The cough doesn't interfere with playing, sleeping, or eating.

- Your child has no fever.

- Your child coughs during the day but sleeps at night.

Croup

Croup is an inflammation of the larynx (voice box) and trachea (windpipe). The inflammation narrows the airway just below the vocal cords. This makes breathing noisy and difficult. Croup can be dangerous because the swelling may cut off the child's air supply. Croup episodes can be scary for both parent and child.

Croup can occur any time of the year, but it's most common between October and March. Some children get croup whenever they have a respiratory illness. Children younger than 3 are most likely to get croup. It's less likely after that age because the windpipe is larger. The swelling is less likely to interfere with breathing.

Signs of Croup

Your child may suddenly begin coughing with a barking sound. Many people think that this cough sounds like a seal's bark. Your child might have a cold that develops into this type of barking cough. The barking sound is the most obvious clue to croup. Most children have a slightly elevated temperature (above 98.6 degrees F or 37 degrees C). Some, however, may have a fever as high as 104 degrees F (40 degrees C).

Your child's anxiety can make croup worse. Try to help your child relax. Sing lullabies or read books while in the steamy bathroom. Let your child lie propped against you, upright on your lap. You may even sleep together in the bathroom. Your child may sense your own anxiety, so try to relax yourself.

When to Call the Doctor

If your child begins coughing that sounds like barking, call your doctor right away. Do this even if the cough begins in the middle of the night. However, immediately take your child to the emergency room if:

- She can't speak because she is so short of breath.

- She seems to be struggling to breathe.

- She makes a whistling sound that gets louder with each breath.

JACK, AGE 16

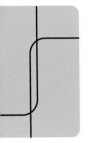

"My girlfriend and I thought Thomas was going to die when he had an attack of croup. It came out of nowhere in the night. We panicked and called the doctor. The shower treatment seemed to help for a while, but we had to do it three times. Finally, I took Thomas outside to the apartment steps. The night air seemed to help."

Treatment for Croup

Most doctors advise the following steps for croup. Take your child into the bathroom and close the door. Turn on the shower at the hottest water setting. Do not take your child into the shower. You are just in the bathroom to have her breathe in the moist, warm air. Stay in the bathroom for about 20 minutes.

The warm, humid air should help your child's breathing. However, she still will have a croupy cough. You may need to repeat the bathroom treatment in the same night. If that doesn't work, take your child outdoors for a few minutes. The cool, moist air may help to decrease the swelling of the larynx and trachea. For this and the next several nights, use a cold-water vaporizer or humidifier in your child's room.

A virus causes croup, so antibiotics cannot treat it. Sometimes doctors recommend decongestants for croup. These drugs unblock the nose or chest during a cold. Some doctors prescribe steroid medicines because they decrease airway inflammation and swelling. Occasionally children are hospitalized.

Prevention for Coughs and Croup
When your child is an infant, keep her away from others who have respiratory illnesses. Make sure the caregivers at day care wash their hands well and often. Teach your child the good prevention habits on page 8.

POINTS TO CONSIDER

What are some causes of coughs? When would you call the doctor for your child's cough?

What is croup? Why might croup worry parents?

What can you do to help your child with croup? When should you go to the emergency room for help?

- After a child's first few months, the most common cause of vomiting is stomach or intestinal infection.

- Dehydration is a serious condition that can result from vomiting or diarrhea. Go to the emergency room immediately if your child is severely dehydrated.

- Diarrhea usually happens because of an intestinal infection. There are ways to keep your child hydrated during diarrhea.

- Constipation can be painful for children. Constipation often can be corrected with diet changes.

CHAPTER 3

Vomiting, Diarrhea, and Constipation

Vomiting

It is important to know the difference between vomiting and spitting up. Vomiting is the forceful throwing up of stomach contents through the mouth. Spitting up is the easy flow of stomach contents out of the mouth. This usually happens with a burp. For more information on spitting up, see the book *Parenting an Infant* in this series.

Vomiting is a reflex action triggered by one or more of the following:

- Chemicals in the blood (such as drugs)

- Stimuli from the middle ear (as in vomiting caused by motion sickness); stimuli are things that cause an action.

- Nerves from the stomach and intestine when the gastrointestinal tract (which contains these body parts) is irritated or swollen

- Psychological, or mental, stimuli from sights or smells

After a child's first few months, the most common cause of vomiting is stomach or intestinal infection. These infections usually are contagious and may produce fever. They also may cause diarrhea, a condition in which normally solid waste is liquid and frequent. Stomach or intestinal infection may cause nausea, or a feeling of the need to throw up. They also may cause pain just below the stomach.

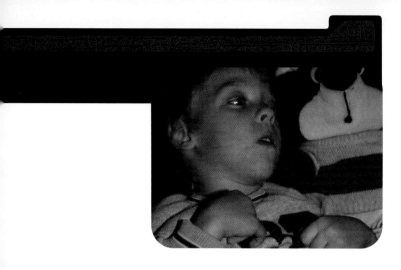

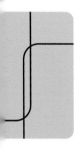

"The first time my 1-year-old threw up, it was all over me. It was nothing like the tiny spit ups she used to do when she was a little baby. She threw up three more times. My mom watched Jessica for signs of dehydration. But Jessica turned out okay. We started her back on foods pretty slowly, just in case."

When to Call the Doctor

Sometimes other types of infections can cause vomiting. These conditions require immediate medical attention. Call your doctor if you see any of the following signs:

- Blood or bile (a greenish liquid released by the liver) in the vomit

- Severe pain just below the stomach

- Swollen abdomen (the area just below the stomach)

- Convulsions (involuntary muscle movements)

- Excessive sleepiness or irritability

- Inability to drink enough liquids

Between the ages of 2 weeks and 4 months, ongoing, forceful vomiting can be a serious condition. It may mean that your child needs surgery. If your child is forcefully vomiting within 15 to 30 minutes after every feeding, call your doctor immediately.

■ Vomiting that continues beyond 24 hours

■ Strenuous, repeated vomiting

■ Signs of dehydration (water loss)

Dehydration

Sometimes a child becomes dehydrated from vomiting or diarrhea. This occurs when the body loses too much water and salt. The right balance of these substances is needed for organs to function. Call your doctor immediately if your child develops any of the following symptoms:

Mild Dehydration	Severe Dehydration
Less frequent urination, or release of liquid waste	(In addition to the signs listed at the left:)
Less activity than usual	Wrinkled skin
Fewer tears when crying	Sunken eyes
Sunken soft spot on the head	Fussiness (easily upset)
Dry mouth	Excessive sleepiness
Weight loss of 5 percent	Cool, discolored hands and feet
	No urination for several hours
	Dark yellow urine

Treatment for Vomiting

Usually vomiting stops without a doctor's help. While your child is vomiting, try to keep him lying on his side or stomach. This reduces the chance that he will breathe vomit into his lungs and upper airway.

Don't feed your child solid foods for 24 hours after vomiting. Children younger than 1 year of age should be given only store-bought electrolyte solutions. These are special liquids that help hydrate the body. You can offer an older child electrolyte solutions or other clear liquids. These include water or Popsicles™. Sugar water is another option. It should consist of ½ teaspoon (2.5 milliliters) of sugar in 4 ounces (118.3 milliliters) of water. You also can use gelatin water. This is 1 teaspoon (5 milliliters) of flavored gelatin in 4 ounces (118.3 milliliters) of water.

The American Academy of Pediatrics (AAP) recommends the following routine after your child has vomited:

1. Wait 2 to 3 hours after your child vomits. Then give 1 to 2 ounces (29.6 to 59.1 milliliters) of cool water. Do this every 30 minutes to 1 hour. Repeat four times.

2. If he keeps this down, offer 2 ounces (29.6 milliliters) of electrolyte solution. After half an hour, offer 2 ounces (29.6 milliliters) of clear liquids. Keep rotating between the two every half hour.

It rarely is necessary to stop breastfeeding when your child has diarrhea or vomiting. Ask your doctor to be sure.

3. If he keeps these down, add half-strength formula or milk (depending on what he usually drinks). This means adding an equal volume of water to your child's usual full-strength formula. Every 3 or 4 hours, increase the quantity of formula or milk slowly to 3 to 4 ounces (88.7 to 118.3 milliliters).

4. After 12 to 24 hours with no vomiting, gradually return your child to his normal diet. Continue to give extra clear liquids.

Diarrhea

A common cause of diarrhea in infants and toddlers is a viral infection called gastroenteritis. The intestine lining contains tiny projections, similar to bristles on a brush. Normally, digested food is made into liquid. This liquid weaves through the projections and gets absorbed into the intestine. When infected, the brush-like lining lets food pass through undigested.

Sometimes children get diarrhea from something new in the diet or from having too much of one food. Colds, respiratory infections, and ear infections also can cause diarrhea. Many young children get diarrhea from antibiotic treatment. Sometimes food poisoning causes diarrhea. Pay attention to any changes that may be the cause of diarrhea. Be prepared to share your observations with your doctor.

Signs of Diarrhea

The stools, or solid waste, of diarrhea caused by gastroenteritis have the following characteristics. They are:

- Frequent
- Watery
- Greenish
- Somewhat slimy
- Foul smelling
- Forceful

When to Call the Doctor

The main concern with diarrhea is dehydration. The signs of dehydration are listed on page 21. If you notice your child becoming dehydrated, call your doctor immediately. Also, call your doctor if:

- Your child loses more than 5 percent of his body weight.
- Your child becomes increasingly sleepy.
- Your child's fever remains high.
- Your child continues vomiting.
- Your child's abdominal pains become worse.

The word *diarrhea* comes from a Greek word meaning "to flow through."

Treatment for Diarrhea

Your doctor decides if diarrhea needs medication. Usually medicine isn't necessary. Never give your child over-the-counter diarrhea medicine unless your doctor suggests it.

Follow these recommendations for diarrhea, outlined by the AAP:

■ Your child may have only a small amount of diarrhea and be active and hungry. He may not be dehydrated and may not have a fever. If this is the case, do not change his diet.

■ If your child has mild diarrhea and is vomiting, offer an electrolyte solution instead of his normal diet. Once vomiting has stopped, gradually restart the normal diet. (See previous section on vomiting for how to gradually restart the normal diet.)

■ Your child may have a watery bowel movement every 1 to 2 hours, or more frequently. He also may have signs of dehydration. If so, call the doctor. He or she may advise stopping all solid foods for 24 hours and avoiding liquids high in sugar. Most doctors recommend giving only electrolyte solution.

■ If your child has diarrhea and you think he's becoming dehydrated, call the doctor immediately. Stop all solids and milk beverages until you talk with the doctor. Offer only electrolyte solution.

■ If you think your child is moderately to severely dehydrated, take him to the nearest emergency room. Give only electrolyte solution until you get there.

When Diarrhea Begins to Improve

Your child's stools may remain loose. That doesn't mean that he still has diarrhea, however. Intestinal illnesses heal slowly. Look for increased appetite and activity, more frequent urination, and the disappearance of dehydration signs. These are signals that your child is getting better.

Your doctor probably will recommend a schedule for getting back to a normal diet. Most schedules look something like this:

- Bottlefed infants not yet eating solids may begin on half-strength formula. Continue giving electrolyte solution.

- Breastfed infants not yet eating solids can resume breastfeeding. Continue giving electrolyte solution.

- Breastfed or bottlefed infants who have begun solids may gradually expand the diet. Begin with applesauce, pears, bananas, and flavored gelatin. If your child has been started on cow's milk, withhold it for 1 to 2 days. Otherwise, follow the recommendations above for breastfed and bottlefed infants.

- Toddlers eating solid foods may begin with applesauce, pears, bananas, and flavored gelatin. Gradually expand the diet to include rice, potatoes, toast, and cereal. Give only small amounts at first. Withhold milk for 1 or 2 days. Continue giving electrolyte solution.

Never give boiled milk to a child. This is especially true for a child with diarrhea. Boiling allows the water to evaporate. This leaves the remaining milk high in salt and minerals. This milk could make diarrhea worse.

Preventing Diarrhea

Most forms of infectious, or easily spread, diarrhea are transmitted by hand-to-mouth contact from exposure to stools. This happens most often in children not yet toilet trained. Teach good hand-washing skills to your toddler. Encourage day care staff to wash their hands thoroughly and often. Avoid feeding your child unpastuerized milk or other foods that may have germs. Avoid giving your child unnecessary antibiotics. Don't give your child unlimited amounts of juice or sweetened drinks.

Constipation

Normally, water and nutrients, or the healthy substances in food, are absorbed as digested food travels down the intestines. The leftover material becomes stool. For soft stools to form, two things must happen. (1) Enough water must remain in the waste material. (2) The lower intestinal and rectal muscles must contract and relax to move the stool along and out. The rectal muscles are located at the end of the intestine. When these muscles contract, they become shorter in length.

Certain foods can lead to constipation. These include:

- White rice
- Rice cereal
- Cooked carrots
- Bananas
- Milk
- Cheese

Constipation results if either function doesn't work. Stool becomes hard and gets plugged up in the intestines. Hard stools cause pain when passing. This sometimes causes babies to hold it in. The longer the stool stays in, the harder it becomes. This means the stool is more painful to pass. Constipation can become a painful cycle.

Constipation refers to how compact the stools are. It also refers to how hard they are to pass. Constipation doesn't have anything to do with how often one passes stools. The frequency and consistency of stools vary according to age and from baby to baby.

Breastfed newborns usually have several stools a day that are soft and mustard-like. Formula-fed infants have fewer and firmer stools. Infants' stools become more compact and less frequent once solids are introduced. Some babies pass stool daily. Some pass it as seldom as every 3 days.

The cause of constipation usually is easy to trace. Often it's the result of something in the diet. New food can trigger constipation. Not having enough water can trigger it in children who have begun solid foods. Constipation also can have emotional causes. Toddlers sometimes get constipated when upset.

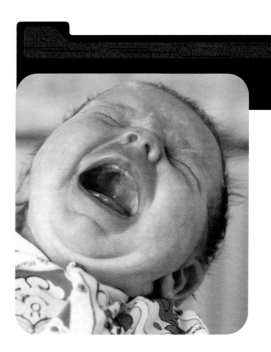

Signs of Constipation

Passing firm stools less than once a day may mean a newborn is constipated. Other signs in older infants and toddlers include:

- Dry, hard stools

- Pain when passing stools

- Abdominal discomfort that is relieved after having a large bowel movement (passing of stool)

- Streaks of blood along the outside of the stool

- Hard, pebble-like stools passed by an infant or toddler who strains during a bowel movement; the child also grunts and turns red in the face during the bowel movement.

- Soiled underpants or diaper between bowel movements

When to Call the Doctor

You may want to call your doctor for advice on treating constipation. Your doctor may tell you to follow a treatment plan similar to the one in the next section.

Laramie Junior High IMC

Treatment for Constipation

The following suggestions can help most cases of constipation. If your child is between 6 and 12 months and has recently begun cow's milk, return to formula. If your child is breastfed, do not substitute formula for breast milk unless your doctor tells you to. Sometimes offering 4 ounces (118.3 milliliters) of pear or prune juice helps to move stools in infants.

RITA, AGE 17

"Mason was 6 months old when he started solids. All of a sudden, his poop changed. I thought it was normal. My older sister saw it, though, and said it looked dry. I realized that Mason was crabbier than usual and kind of grunting. The nurse said to give him a few ounces of juice every day. It worked almost immediately. Now I give him 4 ounces of juice daily."

If your child is eating solids, offer high-fiber foods. These include prunes, apricots, plums, raisins, peas, beans, broccoli, and whole-grain breads and cereals.

Sometimes your doctor may prescribe a laxative or enema. These help soften and move stools. Never use these without your doctor's approval. Always follow the package directions when you do use them.

Preventing Constipation

Become familiar with your child's bowel movement patterns. Pay attention to the size and consistency of the stools. The best approach for children not yet toilet trained is to offer a high-fiber diet. Toilet-trained children can be taught to sit on the toilet after breakfast each day. Give your child a book or toy to relax him. He should try to sit there until he has a bowel movement or for 15 minutes. This bowel training can help prevent future constipation problems.

Sometimes a high-fiber diet and bowel training don't work. It may be that the child is holding in his stools. Talk with your child's doctor if you think this is the case.

POINTS TO CONSIDER

Why is vomiting more serious than spitting up?

Why should parents be careful not to let their children get dehydrated?

How do you know when your child has diarrhea? When should you call the doctor?

Why is it important to become familiar with your child's pattern of bowel movements?

- Poisoning happens often in homes with young children. It is important to have the poison center phone number by every telephone in your home.

- There are procedures to follow if your child has been poisoned. Be familiar with these procedures. There are ways to help prevent your child from being poisoned.

- Burns often happen in homes with young children. Soak your child's burn in cool water before doing anything else.

- You can help prevent burns from happening to your child.

CHAPTER 4

Poisoning and Burns

Poisoning

Most children who get poisoned are not harmed permanently. This is especially true if they receive immediate treatment. However, poisoning can lead to death. Be ready to stay calm and act quickly if your child gets poisoned.

Have the number of your regional poison center near every telephone in your house or apartment. Post it before an incident of poisoning ever happens. This can save time and possibly your child's life. Most telephone books have the poison center's phone number listed on the inside front cover. Staff at these centers answer calls 24 hours a day.

Always keep syrup of ipecac on hand. This substance forces vomiting. Drug stores and pharmacies carry it. Know where your syrup of ipecac is kept. Make sure caregivers know where theirs is kept.

Children get poisoned in their own homes for the following reasons:

■ Products are stored poorly. Leaving bottles on counters or tables is asking for trouble. Purses and diaper bags are other places children look for interesting things.

■ Children imitate adults. They may want to take medicine, clean the house, and spray chemicals.

■ Children are curious. Children learn about their world by touching, smelling, and tasting. Brightly colored liquids and pills and leafy or flowering plants attract children. Spray bottles make children curious as well.

■ Children confuse poisons with safe items. They may think pills are candy. Antifreeze used in cars smells and tastes sweet. Mouthwash may look like a fruit drink.

How to Know If Your Child Has Been Poisoned

Suspect poisoning if you find your child near an open or empty container of a toxic substance. Poisoning is quite likely, especially if your child is acting strangely in any way. Other signs of possible poisoning include:

■ Burns on her lips or mouth

■ Unexplained stains on her clothing

■ Odd breath odors or unusual drooling

■ Abdominal cramps without fever

■ Difficulty breathing

■ Convulsions or unconsciousness

■ Unexplained nausea or vomiting

What to Do If Your Child Has Been Poisoned

Poison can be swallowed or inhaled, or breathed in. Children also may get poison on their skin or in their eyes.

Swallowed Poison. Before calling for help, do the following:

1. Get the poisonous substance away from your child. Make her spit out any from her mouth or remove the substance with your fingers. Keep this material nearby but away from your child. It may help determine what she swallowed.

2. Check for these signs: increased drooling, severe throat pain, difficulty breathing, convulsions, or unusual drowsiness.

If any of these signs exist, call 9-1-1. Or, have someone drive you and your child to the nearest emergency room. Take the poison container and extra poison with you. Do not make your child vomit. This may cause further damage. Do not follow the directions on the container. They may be out-of-date or incorrect.

If you cannot find the poison center telephone number immediately, call 9-1-1 and ask for the poison center.

3. If your child doesn't show these signs, call the poison center. They need to know the following information to help:

    ■ Your name and phone number

    ■ Your child's name, age, and weight. Mention any medical conditions she has or medications she is taking.

    ■ The name of the substance your child swallowed. Read it off the container. Spell it if necessary. Read the ingredients if they are listed. If your child swallowed a plant, describe it in detail. If your child swallowed pills, describe them in detail. Mention any numbers on the pills. Give the pharmacy number and prescription number if the pills were from an unnamed prescription.

    ■ The time you think your child swallowed the poison

You will be given instructions to follow. You may be told to make your child vomit and then go to the emergency room. If so, give her the syrup of ipecac. Then give her a glass of water. If she doesn't vomit within 20 minutes, repeat the dose once. Catch some of the vomit in a container. Bring this container with you to the emergency room for inspection.

Never make your child vomit unless you've been instructed to do so. It may cause worse damage, depending on the type of poison.

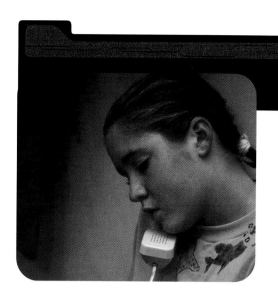

"My cousin once found her child sitting in the middle of a bunch of bathroom stuff. Shampoos, hairsprays, toothpaste—all my cousin's stuff for getting ready. Her toddler had climbed up on a stool and got into the cupboard. My cousin called 9-1-1. They gave her the number of the local poison center. Turns out, Cecily didn't get poisoned. However, my cousin learned to keep her stuff locked up. She also learned to keep the poison center number by every phone."

Poison on the Skin. If your child spills a poison on her body, remove her clothes at once. Rinse the skin with lukewarm, or slightly warm, water. Don't use hot water. If the area becomes red, raised, and/or painful, continue rinsing it for at least 15 minutes. Do this even if your child protests. Then call the poison center for advice. Never use ointments or creams on a burn.

Inhaled Poison. Poisonous fumes can come from an idling car or leaky gas vent. They also can come from wood, coal, or kerosene stoves. Poisonous fumes also can come from mixing household cleaners. If your child is exposed to these or other fumes, do the following.

Get her to fresh air immediately. If she's breathing, call the poison center. If she has stopped breathing, begin cardiopulmonary resuscitation (CPR) (see pages 55–56). Don't stop until she breathes on her own or until someone can take over. Have someone call for help if possible. If you are alone, continue CPR for 1 minute before calling 9-1-1.

Poison in the Eyes. Flush your child's eyes with water if she gets poison in them. Hold her eyelid open with one hand. Pour a steady stream of lukewarm water into the inner corner of the eye. It may help to have another adult hold the child steady. If that isn't possible, try wrapping her tightly in a towel. Clamp her under one arm so you have one hand free to hold the eyelid open. Pour the water with your other hand.

Flush the eye this way for 15 minutes. Then call the poison center. Do not use an eyecup, eyedrops, or any ointment.

Prevention of Poisoning

You can help prevent poisoning from happening. Here's how:

- Poison-proof your home by the time your child begins to crawl. This usually is around 6 months of age.

- Put poisons up high in cabinets that are locked.

- Use child-resistant caps on all potential poisons.

- Always store medications in their original containers.

Burns are divided into three categories. These categories are based on the seriousness of the burn.

First-degree burns are the mildest. They cause redness and sometimes slight swelling of the skin.

Second-degree burns cause blistering and more swelling.

Third-degree burns may appear scorched and cause serious injury to deep skin layers.

- Remind others to be poison safe. Offer visitors to your home a place to put their belongings that is out of your child's reach.

- Teach your child about Mr. Yuk. This green sticker has a nasty face on it. Put Mr. Yuk stickers on all toxin containers as a warning.

Burns

Many things can seriously burn children. Sun exposure, hot water, fire, chemicals, and electrical contact can cause burns. Such burns can cause permanent injury and scarring to the skin.

What to Do If Your Child Has Been Burned

You should act immediately if your child gets burned. This helps prevent further damage to the skin. Follow these steps:

1. Soak the burn in cool water as soon as possible. Run cool water over it long enough to cool the area and relieve the pain. Don't use ice.

Never put butter, grease, or powder on a burn. These home remedies can make such an injury worse.

2. Cool smoldering clothing immediately. These clothes that are burning and smoking with no flames should be soaked with water. Remove any clothing from the burned area unless it's stuck to the skin. If the clothing is stuck, cut away as much of it as possible, being careful not to cut the skin.

3. Cover the burn with a sterile, or germ-free, gauze. This is a thin woven cloth used as a bandage. Use a clean sheet or towel if you don't have sterile gauze.

4. Cover the burn lightly with sterile gauze if it is oozing. Then seek medical attention immediately.

Call your doctor if redness and pain continue for more than a few hours. All burns of the hands, mouth, or sex organs need immediate medical attention. All electrical burns need medical attention as well.

Soak your child in cool water for 15 minutes if she gets badly sunburned. Do this four times a day. Don't dry your child entirely. Leave some water on the skin to evaporate, which will help cool the skin.

Preventing Burns

One way to help prevent burns is to install smoke detectors in all sleeping rooms. Install them in hallways as well. Some people install them in the kitchen and living room. Have at least one smoke detector on every floor. Test all smoke detectors and check their batteries often.

To help prevent your child from being burned, follow these suggestions:

- Lower the temperature of your water heater to below 120 degrees F (48.9 degrees C).

- Keep matches and lighters out of reach of children.

- Don't use worn extension cords or old, unsafe electrical equipment.

- Know the location of all exits in your apartment building.

- Have and know how to use several working fire extinguishers.

- Lock up flammable liquid. These are capable of catching fire easily.

- Avoid fireworks.

POINTS TO CONSIDER

When might you suspect that your child has been poisoned?

What should you do if your child has swallowed poison? What if she has gotten poison on her skin? What if she has inhaled poison?

How can you prevent poisoning from happening to your child?

What should you do if your child has been burned?

How can you prevent burns from happening to your child?

Chapter Overview

- Lacerations are different from scrapes. Lacerations are serious and often require a visit to the doctor.

- Apply direct pressure to the wound for 5 minutes if your child is bleeding. Call your doctor if the bleeding does not stop.

- Many head injuries do not require a doctor's care.

- There are times when you should call the doctor for your child's head injury.

CHAPTER 5

Bleeding and Head Injuries

Bleeding

All children get cuts and scrapes sooner or later. The sight of blood can be upsetting to a young child and to parents. The child may cry or scream. However, the injury may not be serious.

Many injuries to your child's skin simply will be scrapes. This is when the outer layers of skin have been scraped off. There may seem to be a lot of blood if a large area is scraped. It may in fact not be much blood at all.

A cut or laceration is an injury that is deeper than a scrape. There may be heavy bleeding. There may be damage to nerves and tendons.

What to Do If Your Child Is Bleeding

Following is advice on caring for scrapes as well as cuts and lacerations.

Scrapes. First, rinse the scraped area with water. Then, wash it with soap and warm water. Leave the scrape open to air if it is not oozing. If it is oozing, dress it with a large sterile gauze pad. The dressing should loosely cover the skin. Tape it on gently. Sometimes skin sticks to the dressing. You can prevent this by first applying an antibiotic ointment to the skin. Change the dressing whenever it becomes dirty or wet.

Cuts or Lacerations. Try to remain calm. Immediately apply pressure to the site with a clean gauze or cloth to cover it. Keep pressure there for 5 minutes without stopping. If the bleeding starts again after that, reapply pressure and call your doctor. Never use a tourniquet, or tight bandage, on an arm or leg unless you have been trained in its use.

If the bleeding stops, wash the wound with plain water. Make sure the wound is clean. Apply an antibiotic ointment and then cover the wound with a sterile gauze pad. Change the pad when it gets wet or dirty.

When to Call the Doctor

Call your doctor if the bleeding doesn't stop after 5 minutes of direct pressure. Call your doctor if the wound is more than ½ inch (1.27 centimeters) in length or is deep through the skin. Deep cuts can damage tendons and nerves, even if the wound doesn't look serious.

Call your doctor if you think dirt, glass, or other matter is trapped in the wound. Call if you notice any thick, yellow liquid known as pus coming from the wound. Or, call if you notice redness or swelling around the wound. Contact your doctor as soon as possible if the bleeding reoccurs.

Long lacerations or those on the face, chest, and back are likely to leave scars. Usually sutures, or stitches, reduce scarring. However, the stitches should be put in within 8 hours if possible. Call your doctor if you are unsure whether your child needs stitches.

The most common mistake in treating a cut is taking off the pressure too early. Often parents want to peek at the wound. This may result in more bleeding. It also may result in the buildup of a blood clot. This makes it harder to control the bleeding with further pressure. Keep pressure on a wound for 5 uninterrupted minutes.

Preventing Scrapes and Cuts

Scrapes and cuts are difficult to prevent. Children are naturally curious and have many accidents. However, you can do things to minimize the seriousness of injuries. Make regular safety checks in your house or apartment, garage, and yard. Store unsafe items out of reach. Keep all knives, scissors, and glass objects out of your child's path.

Head Injury

A head injury may be a blow to the head. It also can be cuts, scrapes, bruising, or swelling on the head. Most children bump or scrape their head every now and then. Usually it's not serious. However, it is important to know how to recognize a serious head injury.

How to Know If Your Child Has a Serious Head Injury

Children who have only a mild head injury will be alert and awake after the incident. They may cry, but the crying should last no more than 10 minutes. Sometimes minor head injuries cause slight dizziness or nausea. The child might have a headache or vomit once or twice.

Cuts on the head and face will bleed more than cuts on other body parts. This is because large numbers of small blood vessels are in the skin of the head.

BETSY, AGE 16

"I had Lucas 'helping' me with dishes one day. He was standing on a chair at the kitchen sink. I didn't realize how much water he was spilling. He slipped off the chair and hit his head hard. He threw up. I called the emergency room to ask if I should bring him in. They told me to watch him. He didn't throw up again, and I could wake him easily throughout the night. I was so glad he was okay."

When to Call the Doctor

For children younger than 1 year old, call the doctor regardless of the symptoms listed below. Always call the doctor for any serious accident. For example, falling down stairs is serious. Wake your child every 2 to 4 hours for the first 4 to 6 hours after the injury has occurred. Do this to make sure he can be easily aroused. Then, just observe your child for the next 24 hours.

Call your doctor if your child develops any of the following symptoms:

- Drowsiness or increased irritability

- Nausea and/or vomiting more than once or twice

- Difficulty breathing

- Bluish tint to skin

- Unequal pupils

- Inability to move all arms and legs

- Wobbly walk

- Confusion or forgetfulness

- Slurred speech or speech that doesn't make sense

- Persistent headache

- Twitching or convulsions

- Loss of consciousness

- Symptoms that get worse instead of better

- Bleeding that doesn't stop after 15 minutes of pressure

- Crying that lasts for more than 10 minutes after injury

- Weak arms

- Neck pain

A brief, temporary loss of consciousness after a blow to the head is called a concussion. This doesn't have to mean the brain has been damaged. It does mean, however, that the brain's centers for consciousness have been disturbed. Always call a doctor if you suspect your child has had a concussion.

Treatment for Head Injuries

Treat a head injury with ice or pressure if symptoms aren't serious. A large bump on the head probably will go down with an ice pack. Bleeding should stop within 10 minutes if you keep direct pressure on the wound.

Your doctor may request that your child stay in the hospital. Sometimes this is just for observation. Hospitalization is necessary for children who have a severe brain injury or convulsions.

What's the difference between a laceration and a scrape? Why do scrapes bleed so much?

If your child has a laceration, when would you call the doctor?

Would you call the doctor if your child vomited once after a bump on the head? Why or why not?

When is it important to call the doctor after a head injury?

- Choking is a serious safety hazard for infants and toddlers.

- Signs indicate when a child is choking. You must act immediately if your child is choking. You must try to help the child dislodge the item in her air passage. There are procedures for helping.

- You may have to help your child start breathing after a choking episode. You may have to help her heart start beating again. It's best to take a first aid class to prepare for such events.

- You can help prevent your child from choking.

CHAPTER 6

Choking

This chapter discusses how to recognize and respond to the signs of choking in infants and toddlers. This information is not a substitute for a basic first aid class. You should seriously consider taking a class. Doing so can prepare you to save your child's life if necessary.

Choking

Choking is a serious safety hazard for infants and toddlers. It can happen when your child inhales something other than air into her windpipe. Choking means that the child is trying to dislodge, or force out, something that is blocking her airway. It is one of the most common causes of death in children. You must know what to do if your child chokes.

Choking can be caused by liquid that goes down the wrong pipe. Children may gasp, gag, cough, and wheeze. They do this until the windpipe is cleared. This type of choking usually is not harmful.

How to Know If Your Child Is Choking

If your child can cough, cry, or speak and is obviously breathing, the airway is not blocked. However, a child showing the following signs is probably choking and needs your help:

- Gasps for breath

- Is unable to speak or make normal sounds

- Turns blue

- Faints (and you suspect choking)

- Looks like "I'm choking!"

- Drools, panics, eyes get wide

What to Do If Your Child Is Choking

You must act immediately if your child is choking. There isn't time to call the doctor. You will want to follow these instructions or similar instructions you've learned in a first aid class. Be familiar with them before an episode of choking happens.

Child Is Coughing but Able to Breathe and Talk

Let your child cough. Her body is doing its job trying to remove the object from the airway. Never try to remove the object with your finger. This could push it farther back and cause blockage. Help your child relax. Reassure her that things will be okay.

MATTHEW, AGE 18

"My 2-year-old likes to stuff a lot of food into her mouth. I'm used to it by now and just watch her closely. One day at my dad's, she was coughing while eating. My dad was in the kitchen with her. When I got in there, my dad was whacking her on the back, as if that was going to help. I told him to just let her cough. That's what they told us in the first aid class. Sure enough, she was fine in a few seconds. I told my dad he should take a class."

Child Cannot Breathe or Speak and Is Turning Blue

Do not use the Heimlich maneuver you may have heard about. You need a different approach to force an object from the windpipe of an infant or toddler. Be gentle because a child's internal organs are fragile. If you are alone, follow steps 1 through 5 before calling 9-1-1. If someone is nearby, shout for that person to call 9-1-1.

1. Place the child facedown on your forearm in a head-down position. Support your child's chin in your cupped hand, steadying the head and neck. Lay a larger infant facedown over your lap with her head lower than her trunk.

2. Locate the child's shoulder blades. Give five blows to the back rapidly with the heel of the hand between the shoulder blades.

3. If your child still is not breathing, turn her over and place her on a firm surface. Give five rapid chest compressions over the breastbone. Press the chest by placing your fingers one-finger width below the nipple line. Use only two fingers.

4. If she still is not breathing, open her airway by tilting her head back to lift her chin. Do not push her head too far back. This may close the airway in infants and small children. Clear the tongue from the back of the throat by lifting the chin up gently with one hand under her neck. Push down on the forehead with your other hand. Attempt to open the airway by pushing up on the bones at the back of the jaw.

   Look into the throat to see if you can see the object. Do not stick your fingers into her mouth if you cannot see the object. Do not try to pull the object if you do see it. Instead, sweep it out with one finger.

Choking is the most common cause of accidental death in children younger than age 1.

5. If she still is not breathing, try to start her breathing. Do this by giving her two breaths using the mouth-to-mouth or mouth-to-nose-and-mouth technique. (See the next section.) You know the airway is clear if her chest rises with each breath.

6. If she still is not breathing, call 9-1-1. Then follow the steps in the next section.

What to Do If Your Child Stops Breathing After Choking

Sometimes people stop breathing as a result of choking. If this happens, you need to give mouth-to-mouth or mouth-to-nose-and-mouth resuscitation. This means that you try to restart your child's breathing. This resuscitation also is called cardiopulmonary resuscitation (CPR). The AAP recommends the following procedure:

1. Take a deep breath.

2. If your child is an infant, place your mouth over her nose and mouth. Make as tight a seal as possible. If your child is older, pinch her nostrils shut. Place your mouth completely over her mouth.

3. Give two rescue breaths with enough air, so you can see her chest rise slightly. Pause and remove your mouth from hers. This allows the air to escape. Take another deep breath. Do not blow with too much force in infants. This can be dangerous. If no air seems to be getting in, the airway is still blocked. Repeat step 4 from the previous section.

You may find chest compressions on a newborn easier if you encircle the entire chest with your two hands. Do this just below the baby's armpits. Compress the breastbone with the tips of your two thumbs.

4. If your child's chest does rise with each breath, continue to breathe for her. Do so at a rate of about one breath every 3 seconds. Do this until she is breathing on her own.

5. If your child vomits, turn her head to one side. This allows the fluid to drain. Wipe deep inside the mouth with an absorbent towel. However, be very careful not to push the vomit into the windpipe. Suction the mouth if you have a syringe or turkey baster.

6. Check your child's pulse after the two rescue breaths. For infants younger than 1 year old, find the artery in front of and above the elbow. Arteries are tubes that carry blood from the heart to other areas of the body. For older children, find the artery in the neck. It is under the ear and just below the jawbone. If the heart is beating, you should feel a pulse with your fingers touching these points.

ROLANDA AND CLARK, AGE 16

"Our parents paid for us to take a life-saving class. We took it while Rolanda was pregnant. At the time we weren't sure it was important. Now that Aaron is a toddler, we're glad we took it. He puts everything in his mouth. We're ready if anything happens. His day care lady also knows what to do if he chokes. We would choose a different day care if she didn't."

What to Do If You Can't Feel a Pulse

You need to begin chest compressions if you cannot feel a pulse. Begin with your child lying on a firm, flat surface.

1. If your child is an infant, place two or three fingers on the breastbone. Place them one finger width below the nipple line. Press down ½ to 1 inch (1.3 to 2.5 centimeters). Do this at a rate of about 100 times per minute. With an older child, place the heel of one of your hands over the lower third of the breastbone. Press down 1 to 1½ inches (2.5 to 3.8 centimeters) at a rate of 80 to 100 times per minute.

2. After five compressions, give the child one rescue breath. This is described in the previous section. Continue the pattern of five compressions and one breath until you feel a pulse in the artery.

3. If you are alone, call 9-1-1 only after you do 1 minute of this procedure. Then continue this process until help arrives.

Prevention of Choking

Food is responsible for most incidents of choking in infants and toddlers. Watch your child carefully when she eats. There are many ways you can reduce the risk of your child choking on food. Use these guidelines:

■ Avoid raw fruits and vegetables that snap into chunks. Your child can snap off pieces of apples, carrots, and celery. Cut these foods into long, thin strips or slices or grate them.

The U.S. government specifies regulations for toys made for children younger than 3. These toys cannot have parts less than 1¼ inches in diameter and 2¼ inches long. Consider purchasing a device that tests objects for these dimensions. Many children's equipment stores carry these items.

- Avoid serving soft foods that form wads or globs. Peanut butter can choke your child if not spread thinly. (However, it's a good idea to avoid serving peanut butter at all until age 2 or 3. Peanut butter causes an allergy in many children.) A big wad of soft, white bread can choke your child. Using whole-grain breads can help avoid this problem. Raisins in a glob also can cause choking.

- Avoid serving big chunks of food.

- Always watch your child eat. Never leave her unattended.

- Make sure your child sits upright while eating. Don't let your child eat while lying down or while running around.

- Avoid serving hot dogs. If you do serve them, slice lengthwise in thin strips.

- Avoid giving your child nuts.

- Do not give your child chewing gum.

Nonfood items also can choke your child. Young children put everything into their mouth. Keep your home clear of small objects. Choose toys wisely. Know that the following objects often are connected to choking.

- Uninflated balloons
- Pieces of broken balloons
- Baby powder
- Items from trash cans
- Safety pins
- Coins
- Plastic bags
- Marbles

Choking occurs even in safe homes. Be familiar with lifesaving procedures before your child chokes. Take an approved first aid or CPR course. You may save your child's life.

POINTS TO CONSIDER

What would you do if your child started to cough after eating a piece of food?

What should you do if your child is choking? What position is best for your child in this situation?

Why is taking a first aid class important?

How can you help prevent your child from choking?

At publication, all resources listed here were accurate and appropriate to the topics covered in this book. Addresses and phone numbers may change. When visiting Internet sites and links, use good judgment.

INTERNET SITES

The ABCs of Safe and Healthy Child Care
www.cdc.gov/ncidod/hip/abc/abc.htm
Offers an online handbook for people who take care of children

American Academy of Pediatrics—
Immunizations: What You Need to Know
www.aap.org/family/vaccine.htm
Provides detailed information about shots, including why they're needed

The Baby Place
www.baby-place.com
Contains information on pregnancy, birth, and babies

KidsHealth
www.kidshealth.org
Offers information on topics such as infections, behavior and emotions, food and fitness, and growing up healthy

U.S. Food and Drug Administration—
Parent's Corner
www.fda.gov/oc/opacom/kids/html/
parents__corner.htm
Provides articles on giving medicine to children, preventing poisoning and diarrhea, as well as other subjects

USEFUL ADDRESSES

American Academy of Pediatrics National
Headquarters
141 Northwest Point Boulevard
Elk Grove Village, IL 60007-1098
www.aap.org

Canadian Institute of Child Health
384 Bank Street
Suite 300
Ottawa, ON K2P 1Y4
CANADA
www.cich.ca

National Child Care Information Center
243 Church Street Northwest
2nd Floor
Vienna, VA 22180
1-800-616-2242
1-800-516-2242 (TTY)
www.nccic.org

The Nemours Foundation Center for Children's
Health Media
Alfred I. duPont Hospital for Children
1600 Rockland Road
Wilmington, DE 19803

Zero to Three: National Center for Infants,
Toddlers, and Families
734 15th Street Northwest
Suite 1000
Washington, DC 20005
www.zerotothree.org

FOR FURTHER READING

Fairview Health Services. *Caring for You and Your Baby: From Pregnancy Through the First Year of Life.* Minneapolis: Fairview Press, 1997.

Lindsay, Jeanne Warren. *Your Baby's First Year: A Guide for Teenage Parents.* Buena Park, CA: Morning Glory Press, 1998.

Thoennes Keller, Kristin. *Parenting an Infant.* Mankato, MN: Capstone, 2001.

Thoennes Keller, Kristin. *Parenting a Toddler.* Mankato, MN: Capstone, 2001.

GLOSSARY

abdomen (AB-duh-muhn)—the part of the body between the chest and hips

antibiotic (an-ti-bye-OT-ik)—a drug that kills bacteria and is used to cure infections and diseases

cardiopulmonary resuscitation (CPR) (kar-dee-oh-PUHL-muh-nair-ee ri-suh-seh-TAY-shuhn)—a method of reviving someone who has stopped breathing

electrolyte solution (i-LEK-truh-lite suh-LOO-shuhn)—a commercially prepared liquid that helps people who have had vomiting or diarrhea

fever (FEE-vur)—a body temperature that is higher than normal

fiber (FYE-bur)—the part of foods that passes through the body but is not digested; it helps move food through the intestines.

formula (FOR-myuh-luh)—a liquid substitute for mother's milk

gauze (GAWZ)—a very thin woven cloth used as a bandage

immunization (im-yuh-nuh-ZAY-shuhn)—a shot given to people to help prevent a certain disease

intestine (in-TESS-tin)—a long tube extending below the stomach that digests food and absorbs liquids and salt

pulse (PUHLSS)—a steady beat or throb; you can feel a pulse when the heart moves blood through the body.

respiratory (RESS-puh-ruh-tor-ee)—having to do with breathing

sterile (STER-uhl)—free from germs and dirt

stool (STOOL)—the solid waste that the body produces

symptom (SIMP-tuhm)—sign or evidence of a disease or medical condition

Index